The Bipolar Challenge

John Frederick Zurn

Published by Everlasting Light, Yorkville, IL, 2023.

The Bipolar Challenge

by John Frederick Zurn

Everlasting Light Publishing

Yorkville, IL USA

https://www.portalstoinnerdimensions.com/[1]

---

1. https://www.portalstoinnerdimensions.com/

Table of Contents

I would like to express my sincere gratitude to my psychiatrist Dr. Ricaurte. He has been my doctor for over twenty years, and encouraged me to write this book.

Due to his professional guidance and support, I have learned about and grown beyond the limitations of a bipolar disorder.

Introduction

Life can be challenging for everyone, and nobody escapes the struggles of daily life. But for people with mental illness, life can be a roller coaster of fear, anxiety, and despair. Being diagnosed as a person with bipolar and anxiety disorders, my life over the last thirty-five years has been sometimes frightening, often difficult, but also fulfilling.

In the pages ahead, this book describes a few of my personal encounters and work experiences that seek to highlight my own painful growth and development. It also explains some impressions, beliefs, and strategies that have helped me successfully cope with my disabilities, allowing me to "make sense" of my life.

The personal encounters and work experiences I have chosen are as factual and as truthful as I can recall. While sometimes embarrassing, I believe that telling the truth without embellishment, and accurately describing these events, they may be useful to others.

These experiences show how important it has been for me to develop a sense of self-discipline. This includes developing an authentic sense of self-esteem and discovering realistic attitudes in terms of work, routine, and medication. Writing also helps clarify my impressions and experiences, enabling me to better integrate them into my life.

The various ideas I have come to trust and believe in are things that have worked for me over the years. These concepts are a kind of internal structure that helps in day to day living. They have also proven valuable in my relationships with others.

It is very important for individuals with mental disorders to be able to "get into their own heads".

To enhance and support medications, there are many strategies that can be adopted to cope with unique difficulties that many of us face. When our "mental weather" becomes turbulent, it is very helpful to use some or all of these strategies to reestablish a sense of well-being and serenity.

The last part of this book explains some of my beliefs that have brought me contentment and helped me discover my place in the world. In some ways these beliefs are unorthodox, yet everyone's beliefs are original and therefore potentially useful. These beliefs stress my search for certainty in a world of change, and my desire to help others as a way of helping myself find love and fulfillment.

Personal Encounters

My life until twenty was not at all peculiar. I earned pretty good grades in school and participated in extracurricular activities. I went to a lot of "keg parties" - back then the drinking age was eighteen in New York. - I was a "good guy" but not a particularly good person.

At twenty years old, my appendix became inflamed requiring emergency surgery. I then realized that I was totally unprepared for the grim realities of adult life.

Ironically, a few years later, I had my first serious mental breakdown. Thoughts raced out of control causing unsound reasoning. Extreme fear rushed in, and all sense of reality was "tilted". I was hospitalized for about eight weeks, but because the symptoms were strictly manic, I was misdiagnosed.

For a few more years, my situation deteriorated, and I spent time in private and state hospitals. I finally put a knife through my chest and was correctly diagnosed as a person with bipolar disorder. At that time, I received a series of electro-shock treatments that helped lift my thoughts out of the deep grooves of depression.

At this juncture, the responsibility for my mental health became my own. I was prescribed lithium and other medications, and my life improved dramatically. However, I would not take the medicine faithfully, nor would I make a sincere effort to learn about the medications. Ignoring the counsel of mental health professionals, I decided I was "strong enough" to handle my own problems with alcohol and self-effort. Eventually, I neglected to take all medications.

However, when I decided to stop taking my pills, I placed my future in the hands of others. When I became ill, mental health professionals, police officers, and relatives were required to intervene and make decisions on my behalf. Because I didn't believe that I was sick, life became difficult and sometimes harsh as I resisted the needed help. Normal things like housing, food, and jobs had to be started up again from "scratch" once I was well again. All these problems caused my family and friends a great deal of stress and worry.

At this point I will describe a few more of these experiences to help explain how serious and potentially dangerous these situations were at times.

Generally, these episodes took the form of "secret missions". For example, many years ago, I drove my Chevy Nova without paying any attention to traffic signs and plowed into a snow bank. The arresting officers took me to jail and then to Elgin Mental Health Center. For several months my life was reduced to cigarettes, food, and sleeping in the hallways. The constant empty promise became the hope of getting discharged as soon as possible. For most patients, the outside world was overwhelming, so we returned.

Another episode occurred while studying at the university. I became convinced that I was the fifth Beatle. I created a number of meaningless rituals, such as following secret words and phrases in songs. The television set gave secret clues, and other people wore symbolic clothes and "knew" of my plans. For a twenty-four hour period, I watched television with the volume turned off with a record album automatically repeating. I even prepared a "landing strip" so the rock group could land a plane. (I told you it was embarrassing.)

The worst experiences of all were the times I spent in Cook County Jail. One morning, at 2 AM, while I was "secretly" wandering around the streets of downtown Chicago; I suspected that Paul McCartney was giving a rock concert; so I decided to help control traffic, hoping to triumphantly complete my mission. Walking right into the middle of the street, I proceeded to direct traffic. People threw bottles at me from outside bars and a man jumped out of his car and threw me to the ground. When the police officers arrived, I was taken to the Psych Division of Cook County Jail (Cermak.)

It was the most terrifying experience of my life. Prisoners of all kinds were left to wander through the open cells; violence was a constant reality. After about four days, I was simply pushed out the front door barefoot, holding up my pants without a belt.

Shortly afterwards I was at the jail again for about a week. The location of the jail was different but the environment was the same. There weren't separate cells, so it was another chaotic and dangerous situation.

Believe it or not, it took me several more years before I comprehended the dangerous environment of the jail situation. When I finally did understand, I decided to take medication. I not only decided to take medication - I was genuinely afraid of not taking it. My stubborn pride and the belief that taking medication was a weakness had created days, months, and years of perhaps needless suffering.

As I look back at these encounters, I can finally take a lot of the responsibility for them, and I can forgive others and myself.

Work Experiences

Employment can be a difficult issue for people with mental challenges. Getting a job can be an anxious, frustrating experience. Holding on to a job often involves adjusting to new people and routines and coping with the stress of job related situations. There are a number of legitimate reasons why these things are true - the job market, lack of resources, problematic symptoms, low self-esteem and a lack of success in the past.

These challenges can be daunting. It is helpful to see the employment situation for people with bipolar problems as being divided into two parts - getting the job *and* keeping mentally stable. While it is absolutely true that individuals with bipolar disorder can face significant employment hurdles, there are useful ideas that may be relevant to the job scene as a whole.

Let me begin by giving a brief description of my own education and work experiences. I have a B.A. and M.A. in English from Western Illinois University, where I taught freshman composition while I was in graduate school there. My work experience includes teaching at private schools in California and Illinois. For much of my career I have been a counselor at various developmental training centers.

Almost all of my experiences with bipolar concerns "paid off" wonderfully in these work settings. For example, individuals who were dually diagnosed as having mental retardation and mental illness were constantly struggling through a life they couldn't begin to understand. Because of my personal experiences, I was really able to help them. Many of my strategies for solving my own bipolar disorder applied in a broader sense to other disabilities such as autism, mental retardation, and mental illness.

People with bipolar disorders have a vast reservoir of experiences and qualities to draw upon. The amount of courage, patience, and determination that people with mental disorders have so tenaciously acquired, are many of the very same skills employers are looking for. Employers often make hiring decisions based on their "gut feeling". They try to see if they can get along with prospective employees and their current employees. The qualities of compassion and sincerity are highly valued by these employers; qualities that can be hard to find.

A couple of other useful thoughts...

First, the job application and interview process. First, I don't know of a single instance when I have gotten a job by writing down my mental health diagnosis. Even though the application may specifically state that the applicant with mental health challenges will receive special consideration, I believe it actually flags the application from consideration. Second, generally speaking, bringing up mental health issues in an interview, turns an interview into a counseling session.

Looking for work is very hard on the self-esteem of most people. After my interviews, I obsess and replay the scene over and over again. I wait by the phone expecting a return call at any moment. Sometimes I worry about what I might have written on my application, or even if I was too eager during the interview. Worse yet, sometimes I am afraid that an employer will "find out" about something.

In the end, almost everybody has the same or similar worries. Also most interviewees have physical and/or mental challenges of their own. It is also is often illegal for former employers to divulge much information at all. Important to note is that at times jobs are given to people inside the company, although the job must be posted externally. Hiring freezes and an unexpected lack of funding also play a role. For all these reasons, job hunting can make it hard to feel good at times.

For me, keeping a job has been a lot more difficult than finding one. Every few years, I would move to something new. Sometimes there were legitimate reasons like changing my residence. Mostly I taught school and worked as a counselor, as I have mentioned. But many times, stress or some conflict would gradually build up. Unfortunately, I sometimes let situations get worse until it was too much to handle. I was also often impatient and unrealistic about the meaning of success

For almost all of my adult life I have worked, here are a few suggestions about keeping a job. Probably the most difficult thing to manage are medications. All medications have some sort of side effect or other, but if the medication is working well, then sometimes side effects can be dealt with.

For example, physical exercise is very good for weight control, creating a positive sense of well-being, and reducing stress generally. The list of physical activities include: jogging, exercise videos, biking, swimming, yoga, hiking, exercise machines, etc. The trick is to find a form of exercise that can be truly enjoyed. If a person enjoys swimming, for example, they are much more likely to do it on a regular basis.

A couple of other habits that seem simple but are quite important are diet and sleep. Food can influence both energy levels and states of mind. Years ago, I often came home after work and went directly to the fridge. In five minutes, I would nervously eat more calories than an entire dinner. I also caught myself going to the fridge long after dinner, simply because a food commercial was on the TV screen. Food is a constant struggle, and medications make weight gain a real problem.

For me sleep is an even greater challenge. The amount of sleep I get determines my mood to a large degree. Lack of proper rest for me seems to multiply stress, worry, and fears. I have learned to accept it as one of my limitations / challenges.

Returning to medications and work; it cannot be overstated that getting the right prescription, taking it, and believing in its effectiveness, are all important. Some medications are truly effective. This important discovery may help us to tolerate or minimize side effects, so these medications will be more actively and creatively sought out. This can help enhance work related situations and life in general.

Probably one of the more helpful things for surviving work for me is the ability to "leave work at work". When work is finished, I try not to bring it home. This helps about eighty percent of the time. Many times work problems can be left for the next day. This helps me with anxiety and burnout.

Work can be fulfilling, but often isn't. So developing interests outside of work is really helpful. Hobbies like: writing, painting, music, gardening etc. allow for a high degree of creativity that don't rely on others' opinions.

It is useful to make hobbies out of things that have to be done, like chores. Cleaning the house with a favorite CD, doing laundry while using the treadmill, and taking time for doing yard work surrounded by nature can all be relaxing and enjoyable. The chores have to be done anyway, so making them enjoyable helps keep the mind occupied.

One of my biggest problems on and off the job is managing stress. For me, if I am not busy, my mind "turns against me" as worries, imagined fears, and frustration slowly creep in. I obsess over thoughts and feelings, completely distorting situations way out of context and proportion. So I try to stay as active as possible. Some nights I even make a list of activities for the next day. When I wake up, I don't worry about what I'm going to do all day. Sometimes I even incorporate little rewards, and often do my favorite activity last.

So, although it is true that keeping a job and working with medications can be rough, it is also useful to develop personal, overall strategies to help manage work situations and medication challenges. Please remember that throughout these pages, the ideas and suggestions are just that - suggestions. Some ideas will be useful and some will not be appropriate. My life is far from flawless. Like all of us, I do the best I can, but I also have help from others with medications, counseling, and support. I have had this help for my entire adult life.

Impressions

There are a number of pertinent questions associated with bipolar disorder that sometimes generate fear, low self-esteem, and just plain sadness. Probably the most personal question is, "Why me?".

My firm belief is this is a genetic disorder. In my immediate family, there are four of us clinically diagnosed and a number of close relatives who have symptoms. While it is true environment plays a role as well, it seems they appear in families regardless of their environments. Counseling is really important, but in the end, the disorder remains.

For me counseling went something like this: first my parents were to blame; next, when I didn't get better, I was to blame; finally, no one was to blame. If genetics are the source of the illness, it's unrealistic to blame parents, because they too inherited the genes.

Another assumption often associated with bipolar disorder is that it represents some sort of judgment that God has brought down upon the individual. I think the truth is quite different. People grow mostly by taking tiny steps forward throughout their lives. Their ideas and feelings evolve slowly and in limited degrees.

However, individuals who have bipolar disorder are required to grow much more rapidly mentally and even spiritually. Because of their unique experiences, extensive counseling, and a constant search for lasting relief, their lives are often very expansive. While these experiences are often quite painful, provided a stable inner environment prevails, they accelerate development. In my experience a good mental balance sustains about ninety-five percent of creativity and spiritual growth. When I was ill the experiences were about five percent genuine. When I was sick, however, I believed I was at one hundred percent and in a safe inner and outer environment.

I believe that the disorder is both a "blessing" and a "curse". It is a blessing because it enhances creativity, instills compassion, and develops courage. It has often been said that "suffering is grace", and I think there is a great truth in that statement. Suffering is very difficult for me, and sometimes I feel sorry for myself, but life has been much fuller because of it. Perhaps suffering exists for me, and everyone else, because it is the only system that promotes growth. So maybe the question should be: "Why everybody?".

For mentally challenged individuals many challenges are due to others lack of understanding. Since mental illness is difficult to identify and understand, many people think it is not real or else not debilitating. Some believe that it is a weakness or character flaw. Worse yet, some people assert that faith and courage can get rid of the illness. Please don't for one moment believe that lack of faith or cowardice have anything to do with the disorder! I still remember patients in various mental hospitals touching the TV screen in order to be healed. I dare not imagine the number of patients at home who threw away their medication so they could be "saved".

The prejudice and ignorance of some people do make life difficult at times. I remember a woman pharmacist who treated me like a child every time I came in: "Hi. And how are we feeling today?" I also recall situations when several family doctors gave me medicine that adversely interacted with my psychotropic medications. Then there were the high school tours through the state hospitals. Usually a football coach/gym teacher escorted the young co-ed students through the "perilous" corridors. I recall meeting my counselor on the street as he pushed his daughter behind him, so he could protect her.

My favorite memory took place on a city bus in front of Zeller State Hospital in Peoria, Illinois. As I was returning from an institutional pass, I stepped off the bus. A woman with a small child in her lap pointed to the hospital and said: "That's the crazy house. They even have a crazy workshop".

It's a good idea to keep a sense of humor about these situations. I read something very helpful a number of years ago: "Ignorance isn't bliss; if it were more people would be happy".

One final thought about these hurdles - ambition was one of my deep rooted problems that became a kind of curse. Ambition is surely a good thing in many respects but, for me, it became a real problem. Competition with others to achieve success wasn't always realistic. For example, I love teaching, but I can't teach at night; and some teaching situations are too stressful.

I try to remember that it isn't a level playing field. Over time, I have given myself permission to accept the fact that I really have two jobs, as I mentioned earlier. So I am learning to value contentment and happiness despite what our culture promotes.

One of the ideas that I touched on earlier was the need for routines. They are very helpful in ordering and predicting the day's events. Although it is impossible and even undesirable, to plan the day ahead entirely, a general outline helps avoid too many "surprises" that can create anxiety and confusion. For example, putting things off, and procrastination generally, can add unnecessary stress.

This sense of routine includes getting up at a regular time and going to bed at a reasonable hour. This helps the body's biological clock sustain a good rhythm, and encourages inner harmony. These routines can also include completing school and work assignments on time whenever possible, so anxiety is less a part of the process.

However, I have the opposite tendency. I tend to be rigid and have difficulty with change. My obsessive tendency to make mental lists has limited me in some ways. This rigidity sometimes leads to impatience and frustration. It is a kind of perfectionism that seeks to do everything "just right" no matter the circumstances. At times, I try to remember to "lighten up" and realize that most of the time I'm putting the pressure on myself, much more than others are. Routines are really useful, but rigidity can be restrictive.

A useful example of routines and rigidity might be helpful here. Often autistic students are really attached to routines, to the point of having ritualistic behavior. This is true because, I believe, they live in two worlds at the same time - the outer world and the world of their own complex subjective mind. By organizing their outer world with rituals, they are able to help maintain their inner world. When their outer world ceases to feel structured, they can have a difficult time.

For example, one of my students with an autism diagnosis, had a great deal of trouble during a fire drill. This drill occurred late in the day, and when we all went outside, he was really distressed. The disruption of the student's routine was devastating. Additionally, the student's bus was late; also very upsetting. The part of the situation that was truly extraordinary was the student's belief that the fire alarm caused the bus to be late. When it was explained that this wasn't the case, the student began to relax.

There are some minor, yet helpful, similarities between individuals with autism and bipolar disorder that are worth mentioning briefly. A lot of thoughts and feelings run through our heads at any given time. Structure and routine help the inner self flourish because the outer world is stable.

A scientist wrote once that the human mind is like "fruited jello". For many of us, life is more like a rolling wave that can be extremely difficult to dam, divert, or drain. Below, I describe some strategies to help control these waves

For people with mental challenges, it is safe to say, that sometimes life can be awfully difficult. Intrusive thoughts can be hard to ignore. Normally stressful situations for most people are sometimes much more stressful for us on any given day. Physical health issues are often more complicated and harder to diagnose. So leading a "normal" life can be frustrating and sometimes lonely.

Many years ago, a counselor gave me a good suggestion about intrusive thoughts and oddball thoughts in general. He said that having unwanted thoughts is okay, if they come. He recommended that when one foot goes off on its own just gently bring it back to center. In other words, thoughts are just thoughts. This advice helped me become less fearful of the endless thoughts arising in my mind. It encouraged me to talk to mental health professionals and other trusted people when I was feeling frustrated and alone.

Hidden stresses are another frustrating experience for individuals with mental challenges. These problems are rarely experienced by most people, so too often one has to "go it alone". Panic attacks can feel like speeding down an elevator shaft with no cable or bottom. Thoughts can race so fast for a person with bipolar disorder that it feels like running through a burning theater with thousands of screaming people. I remember a friend of mine at Elgin Mental Health Center who told me not to drink the milk because it had LSD in it.

In many ways these experiences are beyond the comprehension of most people, so there is no common frame of reference. It is important to remember that we are all unique, beautiful people who truly live courageous lives.

Physical health issues become more problematic because of additional symptoms and medication concerns. For about a year, I lived in a halfway house in Peoria. One of the residents refused to do chores, so the staff and residents criticized her and constantly complained about her laziness. One day she was taken to the hospital and died the next week of bone cancer. Her diagnosis of depression blinded everyone to her more life threatening health concerns.

Medications sometimes need to be re-evaluated as well, based on changing physical conditions and environmental situations. Individuals with mental health challenges have at least as many physical illnesses as others; the mental health issues create an extra burden most people don't carry.

For all these reasons and more, counseling remains a vital resource for all of us. When I was twenty, a therapist said I would need some form of counseling all my life. I was sure she was mistaken; she was wrong because I wasn't a weak person, nor did I plan to be unstable again. But, she turned out to be correct.

The world is often a difficult place for me to understand. Being a sensitive person, like many people with the bipolar diagnosis, relationships can be extremely complicated. Perceptions of myself and others can be inaccurate. The motivations of people around me are often unclear. Over time, I have needed less counseling, but at fifty-four years old, I still trust the process. Although it is true that there are a few "lunkhead" counselors out there, the majority of counselors are empathetic and knowledgeable.

Counseling has also helped my wife and me better understand my disorders and develop strategies for difficult situations. Counseling has taken a long time because there are almost an infinite number of situations requiring patterns that are useful in a variety of situations.

For example, self-esteem relies on self-confidence. In turn, self-confidence depends upon positive experiences over time, and the ability to be less sensitive in situations generally. In order to accomplish all this, a number of strategies needed to be implemented and tested over time. For example, practical job experiences have created confidence in other work settings, and successful personal relationships have led to a sense of belonging.

Of course, family relationships are often a primary part of counseling. Families are complex and sometimes frustrating. Very few people with bipolar disorder can skip counseling all together, simply because the disorder is often part of the family dynamic. Things like repressed memories and projection (blaming others for all our own problems) can be identified, so individuals can more effectively cope with both the outer and inner worlds. At some point "forgive and forget" is a very healthy attitude.

My parents had seven children in ten years. (My father jokingly said to me once: "You seven children are living proof that the rhythm system doesn't work".) At twenty-five I couldn't even take care of myself, let alone eight other people. Looking back I am amazed how well my parents really did. I can't even begin to thank them for their example of self-discipline, dedication, and self-sacrifice.

Still, counseling is not the total solution. It takes a great deal of courage and self-reliance to persevere in life, especially given the unique challenges many of us face. Almost daily, some situation develops that requires patience and the monitoring of thoughts and feelings. It is helpful to develop a deep trust in the idea that people who are mentally challenged aren't simply struggling with an illness, but rather have a unique way of being. Our lives are purposeful and imaginative.

We're not broken or damaged, we're original. Our lives are not mistakes; our lives are unique expressions of the Creator. We have been given an opportunity to fulfill our lives in many creative ways. For example, at least fifty percent of artists of all kinds have struggled with mental challenges in their twenties and beyond. Many other famous people have lived with this disorder as well.

Abraham Lincoln, for example, was so depressed at times that workers in the White House hid all the knives. Vincent Van Gogh sold only a couple of paintings for a few sympathetic dollars while alive. Now, after his death, just one of his paintings sells for millions of dollars. It is not hard to comprehend his frustration.

There are lists of all types of famous people on the internet. At the end of this book, there is a list of noteworthy people who are associated with bipolar disorder. *(See chapter heading: Some Famous People with Bipolar Disorder)* It's really surprising and encouraging to see how this disorder tends to have the positive aspect of creativity associated with it.

It is the mystery of creativity itself that is perhaps the most fascinating of all concepts related to bipolar disorders. As far as I know, scientists still can't measure it, like they can an I.Q. Nor can many counselors understand the way creativity is present in illnesses. For example, my own episodes had a degree of creativity and original thought. Of course, since I was sick, these experiences were nonsensical or so subjective that they were delusional. Nonetheless, creativity was apparent in some ways.

I can't remember a single time during my hospitalizations when I wasn't given a paper and pencil so I could express myself. I wrote in an effort to express my feelings of anger, fear, and boredom. I understand now that this expression was a pretty desperate attempt to gain control over my mind. After a while, I began writing poetry almost exclusively. It is difficult to explain why I write almost daily, but I'll try.

I write for three important reasons. First, poetry helps me make sense of my experiences, so I can put them behind me. Much of the time, life experiences are difficult to sort out and understand. Beyond the obvious riddles of death, disease, and war; there are personal disappointments and setbacks that are so important or traumatic that they continually engage my mind in an attempt to find answers. These experiences sometimes play and replay for years. When important relationships end, for example, a lot of soul searching goes on in order to resolve any conflicts or loose ends.

Second, the process of writing poetry does a few more things. Each verse of the poem is considered, then reconsidered, so my mind is thinking deeply about it. As the poem progresses, a new awareness about the experience - the subject of the poem - begins to form. Then, when the poem is finished, the experience is seen in a new, more positive light.

Some of my experiences in the mental health system were troubling. (this is probably true for most people with bipolar disorder). I remember writing a poem called "Farewell to Companions" to help me say goodbye to all the wonderful fellow patients that I knew in the state hospital. It helped me to move on.

One of the saddest poems I have written, concerns a woman I sometimes saw at the instituion's commissary while I was a patient at a state hospital. When I first saw her, she had coffee grounds on the corners of her mouth, and she was swinging at imaginary flies with a swatter. Several months later, I saw her transformed into a beautiful young lady. About a year later, after I was readmitted, I saw her again. She was swinging at flies again and she had coffee grounds all over her face. She was also at least six months pregnant, and her pregnancy happened under very suspicious circumstances. By writing the poem "Baby Food" I was able to express my feelings of compassion in a concrete, healthy way.

Writing down thoughts and feelings about my unstable mental states was very helpful in understanding how these experiences fit into my life as a whole. I don't know why, but I think most people with bipolar disorders tend to remember a lot of their unique experiences when they are ill. These often very unusual experiences tned to defy easy explanations. Writing and other forms of creativity can create understanding and closure. In this way, these memories lose their power to dominate the present and future.

In addition to making sense of experience, creative projects are a very good method of self-expression. I believe that our basic nature has a fundamental need for self-expression as an important way to communicate. More importantly, it feels good. It gives a sense of fulfillment which is hard to experience in most other ways.

Seeing an extraordinary nature scene, observing people struggling to change, discovering a new concept in a book, can all be perceived through the window of experience. Then, when the poem, painting, or song is finished, it becomes an original creation. In this world of constant change, creating something that is tangible can be very fulfilling. It also can inspire the artist with faith and devotion.

Self-expression doesn't only apply to writing, painting and music. There are a number of creative endeavors that can be included under the heading of creativity: gardening, woodworking, remodeling, ceramics, photography, film making, acting, calligraphy, mosaics, sculpting, dancing, yoga, etc. Many of these creative activities are offered for a nominal fee at many recreational centers and community colleges as non-credit courses. Group activities offer opportunities for people to socialize with others who have similar interests.

Ultimately, self-esteem in any creative activity is a deeply personal and sensitive undertaking. It is not about success or failure – it is about the sense of enjoyment and fulfillment. I've been writing poetry for a long time. I follow one important guideline: I do not ask others for their suggestions or evaluations. My wife reads every poem, and she only makes supportive comments. This may sound like I'm insecure, but by sticking to this principle, my poems have improved a lot over time.

Once in a great while a poem will be published, and I also self-publish books of poetry. But I always try to write for myself. While it is true that publishing is in the back of my mind, I still write to fulfill my personal need to express myself.

My poetry is often written in rhyme. In the last one hundred years or so, most poems don't rhyme (free verse), so publishers generally don't even accept rhymed verse. This used to worry me about the validity of my own poems. Then one day I realized that poems have rhymed for thousands of years. It put things in perspective. Although, others have countless ways to create, I enjoy writing rhymed poems.

Creativity is more than understanding experience and enhancing self-expression. Creativity can truly take the artist to new levels of awareness. I have come to understand it little by little. It is difficult to explain, but may be described.

Creative expression is like scouting out a new frontier. Sometimes a poem that I have written glimpses at a state of awareness that has not been awakened in my consciousness before. It is like discovering a new land, then returning to my old familiar country. The only difference is when I do return to my country, I have a vague recollection of the experience. For example, when I write a poem about love, I might find a deeper meaning to life. When I write about God, my devotion may take me in a new direction I hadn't previously discovered. This is because the concepts of love and God invite the individual to explore their own inherent creativity.

Faith in the creative process allows glimpses at a new awareness such as intuition. This sense of nonjudgmental consciousness arises because it is somehow connected to the truth of existence. Intuition is often described as a realm beyond thought. It exists as a kind of reservoir of open sky, from which ideas can be crafted. This open space allows for artistic expression and perhaps greater original creativity.

Having said that, it is important for me to explain some other ideas associated with these glimpses at new horizons.

First, these peak experiences usually offer only a modest glimpse of their underlying meanings. After a few brief moments, the mind almost always immediately returns to the difficult task of daily living. The presence of the new awareness may not be fully understood for years.

Secondly, I cannot express strongly enough that these experiences are not meant to be an escape from the challenges of everyday life. They do not take the place of medications, routines, counseling, etc. My own experience has taught me, sometimes harshly, that any experience gained in discovering deeper levels of awareness, has been lost or totally fragmented by careless attitudes and risky behavior.

All the things I do to remain mentally "well" and physically healthy are the real reason these experiences surface at times. Self-discipline, self-control, and perseverance are useful attitudes required to map out and explore new frontiers.

While creativity encompasses the whole of experience, my writing has been at its peak when my behavior has been prudent, and my mind has been stable. When I was unstable, writing and living seemed very creative at times, but really were unintelligible.

In closing this section on creativity, a few words about the relationship between intoxicants and creative expression. I was a heavy drinker for many years. In fact, when I was nineteen, I was driving a mustang eighty miles an hour, drunk with three other people in the car. I barely avoided an accident that would have probably killed all of us, as well as the occupants of the oncoming car. I always thought I wrote better and was generally more creative when I was intoxicated. But it just wasn't the case. After completely giving up alcohol about twenty years ago, my writing has really improved, and, at times, my poems help me glimpse at those peak experiences.

Finally, these are my attitudes about risky behavior and my belief in medication. I read once that if someone doesn't care about themselves, then at least, they should care about the inconvenience they cause others, when they doesn't take care of themselves. For example, if I decide to quit taking medication, and I'm unable to sleep entirely, I will undoubtedly get very sick. Then, my wife will have to take care of me and worry about me as well. So, by caring about my own health I don't leave it for others.

This culture often doesn't understand the lives of people with mental challenges, and maybe never will. The media also have trouble with prejudice in story lines and in comedy, encouraging stereotypes and misinformation. But, I decided a long time ago that I would take the medication for my own well-being and as an exercise in humility. I try to remember that some of the greatest sages ever known are celebrated for this very quality.

Beliefs

It is very difficult for me to discuss my personal beliefs because they are apt to be misunderstood, or worse, met with ridicule and disrespect. Because of this, and the problem of conceit, I have almost never shared my beliefs with anyone.

I have always respected the beliefs of others and strongly support the view that every religion has truth at its core. So, I never intentionally criticize the beliefs of others, nor arrogantly state my own views are preferable or correct.

Everyone has the legitimate right to their own beliefs, and I sincerely respect them as a way to God. Some compassionate people with very orthodox religious views were very, very good to me – taking me into their homes as a place to live, providing love and support, and even bailing me out of Cook County jail.

While my views are pretty unorthodox they may be reassuring and, perhaps, useful to share. Due to the unique experiences of people with a bipolar disorder diagnosis, we have needed to sometimes "think outside the box" when it comes to grappling with mental health issues and life generally. This original thinking has led us to ideas and perceptions that are sometimes spiritually expansive.

My most deeply held belief is that God exists. God exists everywhere, not as a bearded judge on a cloud, but as the Light and Love within and throughout creation.

I remember when the Russians first orbited a man around the earth. A cosmonaut reported, triumphantly, that he couldn't find God anywhere up in space; therefore, God didn't exist. This has been the attitude of many scientists. If God isn't tangible to our senses, then he must not exist.

We can't see electricity, yet it exists. We can't see the wind, only its effects, yet it exists. Often I believe scientists, professors, and others, work diligently to earn PhDs in physics, chemistry, and sociology, but their understanding and experience of religion ends with high school or even earlier. A teenager's understanding of God may seem irrelevant to one who has studied astrophysics for many years.

The concept of God is mysterious and doesn't exactly yield to logic. It defies attempts to be marginalized or trivialized. It is my belief that all great religions have a deep sense of intuition and power at their centers; when politics, fanaticism, and histories are seen in perspective, the scriptures of these religions all hold very similar ideas about truth. Even though they are cloaked in different customs and languages, they can all lead to growth and peace of mind. This has been my view for a number of years now.

Like many people, my religious views have evolved over time based on: studying and practicing religions, observing and experiencing life, and occasionally awakening to spiritual knowledge. This evolution involved a constant "falling on my face," picking myself up, and starting over. It has always been challenging and, at times, took a measure of courage and faith. This evolution continues. Since spiritual pride is one of my major character flaws, I will not describe any of these experiences directly; instead I include some of my poems at the end of this book.

My first serious encounter with spiritual matters was intrinsically linked to my initial struggles with the onset of bipolar issues. For many of us, the symptoms created a kind of "spiritual crisis" because we didn't have any understanding of what was happening to us.

During one such crisis, I imagined I could find God by racing my thoughts as fast as possible. I didn't fully realize what I was doing, of course, but years later I figured it out. The consequences were terrifying. The psychiatrist called the symptoms signs of "religiosity" which means an unhealthy attachment to religion. In other words, I was using religion to solve all my problems.

This fixation on religion continued for a number of years and took humiliating turns. Sometimes I believed I was Christ, and that I possessed magical powers. Other times I begged for money on the street. Once a man put a gun to my head, when I walked into a bar, and tried to talk to him.

These delusions and behaviors were all evidences of my illness, but the counselors never truly considered that I was actually seeking genuine spiritual experiences. How could they, when I was so sick?

It would have been very helpful if someone had introduced me to a form of fulfilling worship. I think sometimes, individuals with mental illnesses do not simply desire to return to the life they have known. They seek growth and change. They do not necessarily want to tear down their outer life, rather they really want an expansion of their inner lives. In my case, however, I'm not sure I would have listened at the time.

It is easier now, but forty years ago, most religious encounters didn't promote this kind of expansion. It wasn't until I read a book about meditation that I began to develop a sense of inner quiet and purpose that helped me actively attempt to control mood swings. Meditation has been, and continues to be, essential for my spiritual growth and mental stability. In the section titled *Stress Relieving Strategies*, I describe some basic meditative methods.

Every religion has its "mysteries" and practice some form of meditation in their quest for divine knowledge. These days, descriptions about their ideas and practices are widely available. For example, an internet search with a key word like 'religious practices' lists sites with many useful concepts related to meditation and religions in general.

Basically, meditation is slowing and clarifying of thoughts. It is a great companion to medication. They work together to calm the mind, rest the nerves, and, over time, lead to insights regarding life.

Meditation is very helpful for all kinds of creative endeavors. It provides a deep level of concentration, a high degree of sincerity, and a source of inspiration. I've been meditating for more than thirty years. It has made all the difference especially when my other pillars of strength get wobbly because of stress, mood swings, and physical health concerns.

For me, God is not a judge who punishes me when I make mistakes. My conscience is the inner sense that teaches me this. God is everywhere. He is behind creation like the flip side of a coin or the back of a piece of paper. God is like a movie screen while a movie is showing. When the theater patrons watch the film (the world), he sees the movie. But behind the movie is the ever present screen (God).

God is the director of the cosmic drama. He directs the play and plays all the parts as well. So in one sense, simply stated- everything in creation is divine. We are all divine, as are the trees, rivers, and sky, the entire natural world. This belief about God is common in parts of Asia, and many Native American cultures.

To use a couple more another metaphors..

Creation is a glass of salt water. The salt is invisibly dissolved in the water. Yet, it can be tasted. Water can be ice, water or steam. So, the notion that "seeing is believing" that so dominates many aspects of modern thinking, is limited in many ways.

It's a little like the story of the lost watch. There is a watch lost in the bushes, but there is a street light down the road, so the search for the watch is carried out under the light. The watch isn't there, of course, but there's more light under the street lamp.

As Jesus stated: "The kingdom of God is within", a similar idea running through many religious traditions. God is not found looking everywhere outside in the world so much, as He is to be found within all of us. Every religion seems to state this truth in some way or another. The external world cannot provide permanent happiness. Since it is constantly changing, it ultimately disappoints.

God is not only permanence, God is Love. He doesn't "possess" Love as a quality or virtue. God is Love itself. God doesn't create suffering, in fact God helps transition suffering into happiness, dissatisfaction into contentment, selfishness into service, and doubt into faith. He doesn't view us as sinners, unworthy of grace and mercy.

Unquestionably, the most difficult idea for me to overcome was the notion that, if I didn't believe and behave in certain ways, I would go to hell. But, for me, the path led in a different direction. It has often been said that there are many paths up the mountain, and many rivers to the sea. This is now my belief as well.

I have come to believe that the search for meaning and certainty in life is always within us in some form or another. No matter the activity, it is motivated to some degree by the spirit, even if the search is seems odd. A drunk may be seeking happiness or searching for meaning. A miser may be seeking stability or independence, and a dictator may be seeking control of the future. In fact, I believe almost every activity is an attempt to connect with the spirit of God. It is like the moth rushing toward the flame except the flame is really Love in the form of Light.

The next question that arises for me is : Why does this situation of endless searching exist at all? Why isn't life filled with contentment and peace? The surprising answer is found in many scriptures.

Put simply, desire is the cause of all kinds of dissatisfaction and suffering. From the time individuals rise in the morning until they go to bed at night, their minds are ceaselessly in motion. It has been said that the "average" person can go without thinking for about seven seconds. The mind is like a caterpillar that can't move from one leaf until it has grasped another one.

Buddhist scripture sometimes describe this concept of mind as a fish out of water endlessly flopping on the sand. Hindu scripture describes the mind as a monkey in a cage acting wildly after it has been stung by a bee. The point is, the mind is exceedingly difficult to control, and that thoughts are the source of most worries, fears, and discontentedness.

To carry the point further, thoughts are like a ball of yarn with many different kinds of thread. If every thread is removed, the ball of yarn ceases to exist. At any given time, when thoughts are gone, the mind is gone also. The mind (not the brain) is a bundle of thoughts.

This energy called consciousness exists without the mind, not the other way around. So, by slowing the thoughts, the mind begins to quiet. That is why adults tell children to take deep breaths when they are upset. The slower the breath, the slower the thoughts, and so in turn, the quieter the mind.

Controlling the mind with some form of discipline is so helpful for people with bipolar issues. Disciplining the mind helps minimize unstable thoughts and can enhance inner growth. It is a way to gain more control of the sometimes challenging thoughts that are bothersome, especially when we are doing everything else that we need to be doing.

Much of the time (but not always) thoughts are a source of discomfort and dissatisfaction. For me, a main source of dissatisfaction is my constant need to compare myself to others. It can be labeled conceit, ego, pride, or selfishness, but it almost always leads to discontent and anxiety.

For example, let's say I have job that pays well, and the coworkers are great. I am content and enjoy the work. Then my brother calls me and informs me that he just got the same kind of job for twice the pay. My tendency would be to instantly find flaws with my own job and contemplate the unfairness of the situation. By comparing my brother's pay with my own, I become frustrated and unhappy.

Another example of this tendency to compare... This is a true story. I worked in the receiving department of my family's hardware store for several years. We had an expensive snow blower for sale, a machine designed for mostly estate and commercial use. One wintry day, a customer bought one, and when we delivered it to his house; it barely fit in the garage. In fact, it was wider than the sidewalk. As we were leaving, he brought it out and pushed it out into the driveway so the neighbor across the street could see. The neighbor had a very similar snow blower with an identical sidewalk. I know "keeping up with the Jones'" is a cliché, but it is also points out the problems of pride and pointless competition.

In many ways, this obsessive need to compare is a source of frustration and anxiety for me. When I see others drinking, I become despondent. If I hear about a relative's success, I get discouraged; and whenever I have a difficult day, I get irritable and blame others.

So why *do* I compare myself with others? Are they battling with a major disorder that is not their fault? Have they had to give up unhealthy activities? Do their moods affect their relationships on an almost daily basis?

There is no way to accurately compare the lives of people *with* mental health issues to the rest of the population. Most of us spend our lives with an "elephant strapped to our backs". So, comparisons are pretty deceptive.

But here is a nice surprise. All the things that most individuals with bipolar disorder have to give up, are the very things that are truly advantageous for spiritual growth. Things like no alcohol, no all-night outings, and no excesses generally are the very things that most people cannot do. The constant wrestling with the unusually perplexing states of mind are also things that others only rarely deal with, if at all. So, for me, bipolar problems have required me to be a better person and a more active seeker. Without this disorder, I seriously doubt that I would have become a spiritual person at all.

All of us are uniquely spiritual in our own way. There is no single "right" answer. God is infinite, and if everyone is made in God's image, then we are, in fact, infinite. Any sincere path can lead to a deeper faith, provided Love is the guiding light.

It has been my experience that God is not male. For me, God is much more closely understood as female. This infinite power called God has been so often described as male that even in poetry God is described as "He". God is beyond the perfection of male and female.

Finally, the experiences of many individuals with bipolar disorder, create feelings of alienation and loneliness. So, it *is* important not to use beliefs, practices, and religion in general, as a reason for isolating ourselves from everyday activities. For most of us, the trick is to juggle and balance all the roles and activities of our lives in such a way that healthy growth and realistic achievement are measured in our own eyes, and by our own standards.

Conclusion

I'd like to thank the readers of this little book, who have followed along with me, as I have described these experiences and beliefs that have so shaped my life. I have no doubt that you have your own story as well. Hopefully you can understand my frustrations and identify with my fears, in the light of your own experiences. Although our story lines are different, I suspect many of the themes of our lives are very similar. Thanks again for caring.

I'd also like to thank my relatives, all the mental health professionals, friends, and teachers who have helped me along the way. It seems that I learned something valuable from each one. I owe them all a lot.

In the following pages, I describe a variety of specific strategies that I have used successfully throughout my adult life. They are not complicated. I use most of them to this day.

I have included a list of famous individuals who now have or have had bipolar disorder issues. After that, there is a pretty good list of accessible resources that further explain the topics in this book.

At the end, I have added ten poems about my mental illness experiences, and another ten poems related to things of the spirit. I hope you enjoy them.

>> 7 Stress Relieving Strategies <<

In the following pages are some methods of reducing stress, managing symptoms, and enhancing spiritual growth. *They are meant to be used together with medication, counseling, and a sensible lifestyle.*

It is important to note that these strategies are not meant to be used while driving or practiced repeatedly within a very short period of time.

Please take what you can use and leave the rest. I heard a wise saying years ago: "Be like the wise ant. Take the sugar and leave the sand". This saying has been very helpful to me in many situations. I hope you find some of these strategies helpful as well.

Strategy 1 : Counting Steps

This meditation is an excellent way to train the mind to focus on a given task. I have practiced it for many years while jogging or using a treadmill. It can be adapted for activities like walking, running and bicycling. This strategy has kept my mind from wandering and strengthened my concentration. I use it to dissolve annoying thoughts and feelings of sadness. As a it helps me jog and walk for longer periods of time and makes the treadmill easier to use on a regular basis.

For this activity I repeatedly count my steps, alternating left and right:

1 Right Step 2 Left Step

3 Right Step 4 Left Step

5 Right Step 6 Left Step

7 Right Step 8 Left Step

Begin again at 1

Strategy 2 : Guided Meditation

Guided Meditation usually takes the form of an audio recording played back electronically or an in-person setting with a facilitator. This meditation creates an atmosphere of relaxation by using natural sounds, specific colors, peaceful music and the soothing voice of a person who "guides" the listener. These can be excellent, and I have found them to be very helpful.

One of my favorite guided meditations is called <u>Rainbow Butterfly</u> by Emmett Miller. It is quite famous. I have recommended it to relatives and friends. (See section named "Resources") Like most forms of relaxation and meditations, it is probably a good idea to practice a couple of times a week, even when things are going great, so when a difficult day develops, the materials are already familiar to you.

Strategy 3 : Visualization

Visualization is almost synonymous with guided meditation, except visualization can be practiced without an audio recording or a facilitator. I often use visualization when I have trouble falling asleep. I lie in bed and imagine myself in a country setting. I study the houses and streets and try to find things that "need" to be done like cleaning, painting, and construction projects. Sometimes I count the lumber and bricks that are loaded on to a wagon. I see myself carefully sweeping; I mix cement and so on. As I do each chore, I pay particular attention to all aspects of each task. This occupies my mind, so I forget everything else. It usually works.

Strategy 4 : Affirmations

Affirmations are positive statements, often memorized, and repeated many times to create a positive attitude and/or change problematic behavior. They are meant to replace feelings of despair and helplessness with more positive emotions.

Affirmations can be long or short, general or specific, material or spiritual.

Below are two examples written by an Indian yogi named Paramahansa Yogananda from *Scientific Healing Affirmations*, pg. 51, and one that I use often.

> I relax and cast aside all mental burdens, allowing God to express through me his perfect love, peace, and wisdom.

> As I radiate love and goodwill to others, I will open the channel for God's love to flow to me. Divine love is the magnet that draws to me all good.

<u>I try to remember to use this when a situation becomes difficult:</u>

The greatest auspiciousness is courage.

The greatest deed is mercy.

The greatest weapon is patience.

The greatest happiness is contentment.

Strategy 5 : A Basic Meditation Method in 4 parts

This is the meditation I have used for many years. It is a lot easier to practice than it seems. The whole method can take as little as fifteen minutes and is done silently.

I created it out of desperation, and it is a synthesis of several methods. To begin, it is helpful to sit in a chair or lie flat on your back, so the spine is straight. Then take a few deep breaths. Then move to silently counting the in-breath and out-breath:

Part A : Counting the Breath

breathe in 1 breathe out 2

breathe in 3 breathe out 4

breathe in 5 breathe out 6

breathe in 7 breathe out 8

Begin again at 1

Repeat for about 5 minutes.

Part B : Categorizing Thoughts

Thoughts fall into four basic categories:

Memories

- thoughts about the past

- It rained yesterday.

Planning

- thoughts about the future

- My rent is due tomorrow.

Imagining

- thoughts about imagination

- What rhymes with star?

Thinking

- any thoughts you can't categorize.

Part C : Counting *and* Categorizing

After counting the breath in, identify the thoughts as they enter the mind with breathing in and out the four thoughts:

breathe in breathe out

me mories

pla nning

ima gining

Part D : Breathing and a Meditative Word

Finally, a meditative word is repeated silently as is the rest of the meditation. For example, "Amen" is a meditative word:

breathe in breathe out

ah men

ah men

Strategy 6 : Tackling 4 Difficult Thought Patterns

Thought patterns are like trains that run along the tracks of the mind. These trains have some basic characteristics despite the circumstances. The following patterns are some of my most troublesome: *obsessive thinking, concentration problems, catastrophic thinking*, and sometimes *panic attacks.*

1 : Obsessive Thinking

For me, obsessive thinking includes the replaying of problems and work assignments in my head. For example, if I have a lot of chores to do, I organize them and reorganize them until my mind is satisfied. If that order varies because of unforeseen circumstances, it can be difficult for me.

There are a couple of things that I try to do to help me. First, I write down a list when I have chores to do, or when I go to the doctor for example. With all the information written down, it is easier to let go. This also works for interpersonal problems. If I write it down in some detail, and describe how I want to solve it, then I can let it go much of the time.

Another thing I really try to do is keep myself busy. When my mind is actively engaged in some activity, the obsessive thinking seems to fade away. In fact, the more free time I have, the more I usually obsess. This obsessive thinking remains a problem for me, but the ability to identify it has helped.

2 : Concentration Problems

My problems with concentration have varied based on different situations which I have had to cope with over the years. There was at least one time when I couldn't concentrate at all, and it was especially frustrating when I tried to read something. So I did something very odd. I began to very discreetly read children's books. I started with the most elementary, then, worked my way up, until I could read almost normally in about a week.

However, for concentration generally, all kinds of activities (including other reading strategies) are much more productive than leaving the mind with nothing to do.

The method of "Counting Steps" and "A Basic Meditation" have proven very helpful as well.

3 : Catastrophic Thinking

The next difficult thought pattern is catastrophic thinking. For many years, my mind engaged in this kind of thinking, and I didn't even realize it. For example, let's say that I have misplaced my keys. First I assume someone has stolen them. This thief then could steal my car or get into my house. He might then get my personal information and commit identity theft. Finally, I could be ruined financially.

There are really two points here. First, perhaps in the past you have had some terrible problems that have spiraled down into a very difficult place. But that is not what is happening now. The past does not *cause* the present or future.

Second, understanding that the mind is engaging in catastrophic thinking is helpful because the pattern is recognized. Sometimes I talk to my wife about it and that helps. Often an empathetic listener can be helpful. (By the way, in the example of the lost keys: I usually find them in my jacket).

4 : Panic Attacks

Finally, panic attacks are the most difficult thoughts of all for me. First I use the tools I have available: exercise, meditation, guided meditation, and positive thinking. If these don't work, I try to detach my thinking from the energy, so the feeling is there without the panicky thoughts. But the truth is, I usually take medication. I used to go for hours "sticking it out" but it was stubborn and silly.

It is important to emphasize the power of medication, counseling, and resourcefulness when struggling with burdensome moods and troublesome thought patterns. A number of years ago I fractured my ankle, but didn't realize it was broken for a couple of weeks. When I finally found out, I couldn't believe how much easier it was to suffer physical pain when compared to mental anguish. It has really helped reinforce my beliefs about medication.

Strategy 7 : Chanting, Prayer, Yoga, Inner Sound

Chanting

Chanting involves singing spiritually charged words and phrases in a repeated pattern. For example, Gregorian Chants use sacred words that are sung. These chants are another way to calm the mind, but they also help improve mood and outlook.

Krishna Das, an American who studied in India, is one of the better known performer of Hindu chants in America. Here is an example of a Hindu chant: Sri Ram, Jai Ram, Jai, Jai, Ram. This chant is a scared hymn to Lord Rama. (pronounced: Shree Rahm, J-I Rahm)

Prayer

Prayer is perhaps the most widely understood of all forms of worship. It can be very reassuring when it is sincere. A potentially powerful prayer is The Roman Catholic Rosary, because it is a form of meditation.

My problems with prayer stem from lack of gratitude, pride, and impatience. Whenever something good happens to me, I want something more, instead of being grateful for what I have been blessed with. My sense of pride creates the feeling that I don't need help regardless of the circumstances. In addition, my lack of patience doesn't allow me to take my time to pray in a sincerely humble manner by praying from the heart. So when I do pray, I have to remove all the obstacles my thoughts create.

Yoga

This is the practice of yoga postures (asanas). Yoga has recently flourished in the west and is taught in many, many places. In addition to being good for overall health and well-being, when combined with meditation practices, it is a spiritual path for many. It can be practiced alone or in groups. With Yoga, less is sometimes more. Probably most yoga instructors caution against trying to master difficult postures before the student is ready. Some yoga students get hurt or discouraged, when they unnecessarily push their bodies. Start with beginner practices and gradually grow into more difficult postures.

Inner Sound

Inner Sound is a form of meditation that is easy to understand but difficult to practice. It involves listening to a sound like water, bells, and even listening to the mind itself. As the listener concentrates and continues to "hold on" to the sound, other thoughts and feelings dissolve. The famous Tibetan singing bells are an example of this form of meditation.

Resources

These resources have been very helpful to me over the years. It is probably a good idea to use them when things are going well, so they can be used effectively as needed. I have also included only those resources with which I am pretty familiar. Again, these works below are not a substitute for medication and counseling, but they have been very effective for me as a part of an overall support system.

Books

The Bible: The New Testament

It has 27 books. Much of it centers on the life on Jesus Christ.

The Dhammapada

This book was written by the Buddha and is one of the most important books in Buddhism. It deals specifically with the mind, and it can be read in a couple of hours.

The Bhagavad Gita

This book offers a very different view of the world than that of the west. It is part of India's epic, *The Mahabarata*.

The Mahabarata

One of the 2 epic tales of India, the story of the Pandava brothers.

This book can be read in a couple of weeks.

Journey of Awakening

As a kind of meditator's handbook, this easy to read book was written by Ram Dass, formerly known as Richard Alpert- a Harvard psychologist. It offers practical ways to find contentment and joy. This book is also very well known.

Lives of the Saints

This entry represents a general title for books about saints of all religions. The lives and writings of saints often give a sense of purpose and direction for those on the spiritual path.

Guided Meditation

There are many audio recordings that help the listener develop a sense of deep relaxation. They can be particularly good when the stress of daily life becomes overwhelming.

Rainbow Butterfly, by Dr. Emmet Miller

https://shop.drmiller.com/heal-your-body/rainbow-butterfly/

Side A https://www.youtube.com/watch?v=Dc8w_By5Jnc

Side B https://www.youtube.com/watch?v=QqFhqRVeKgM

Chakra Balancing and Energizing, by Dick Sutphen

https://www.youtube.com/watch?v=uygwxcqtxl4[1]

Music

Chants: All religions use music and chant as a way of balancing thoughts and feelings.

Gregorian Chants: These chants are centuries old.

Hindu Chants: Krishna Das is probably the most widely known Hindu chanter. But there are many, many, more.

New Age Music: Music of this genre is often used in therapy, hospitals, care centers, and almost everywhere else. Some examples are: Enya, Deuter, Halpern, and Ed Van Fleet.

---

1. https://www.youtube.com/watch?v=UYGWXcqtXL4

Recordings Audio recordings and film can be an excellent way to learn about other cultures and religions, without trying to read through an ocean of difficult books. The Catholic faith has many, many audio recordings that focus on various saints.

Books / Groups

Finally there are also a wide variety of information in specific libraries and the internet. There are also many religious groups that exist all over. Sometimes they can be hard to locate, but they are usually open to visitors when you do find them.

Some Famous People with Bipolar Disorder

Buzz Aldrin (astronaut)

Ludwig Beethoven (composer)

Tim Burton (artist, director)

Dick Cavett (television journalist)

Winston Churchill (politician)

Charles Dickens (author)

Patty Duke (actress)

Ralph Waldo Emerson (author)

Carrie Fisher (actress)

Linda Hamilton (actress)

Jimi Hendrix (musician)

Ernest Hemingway (writer)

Herman Hesse (writer)

Chris Kanyon (wrestler)

John Keats (poet)

Cynthia M. Sabotka (author)

Robert Schumann (composer)

Britney Spears (musician)

Michael Spensieri (lawyer, politician)

Ben Stiller (actor)

Daryl Strawberry (baseball player)

Sting (Gordon Sumner) (actor,musician)

Ted Turner (businessman)

Mark Twain (author)

Jean-Claude Van Damme (actor)

Jennifer Lewis (actress)

Isaac Newton (scientist, mathematician)

Florence Nightingale (nurse)

Jane Pauley (TV journalist)

Edgar Allan Poe (poet, writer)

Charlie Pride (musician)

Theodore Roosevelt (president)

www.realmentalhealth.com/bipolar/bipolar_celebs.asp

Poems

Farewell My Companions

When horses stampeded within my sick mind,

You held my hand tightly and helped me unwind.

When demons possessed me and anger took hold,

You knew how I felt without being told.

When life was oppressive with dark thoughts of death,

You asked me to linger and helped me find rest.

When experts gave up and left me alone,

You shouldered my burden and made it your own.

My words can't express my feelings inside;

Without your affection I might well have died.

Although I have left you, I still hear you call.

Farewell my companions. Good-bye to you all.

Remember I love you and feel you within,

Farewell my companions. My new life begins.

Baby Food

Mary Doe spent her afternoons

in the Elgin State Commissary.

Her hand me down clothes

and coffee stained mouth

matched her dirty blonde hair

and half crazy talk.

She often would dance

from table to table

swinging a used fly swatter

over her head.

I was there too

killing the time

and bolstering my confidence

by chugging black coffee.

We never met

because mentally ill people

often ignore each other

lost in their own psychosis.

But, by late spring,

I saw her become

more sane

and she was truly radiant.

I was released to the street

that spring,

but it didn't take,

so I returned.

I was soon back in the commissary

slugging down coffee.

I was shocked,

when I saw her there pregnant,

dancing nonsensically

and swinging the fly swatter in the air

again.

Too horrified and curious

to let it go,

I asked a friendly tech

what went wrong.

It seemed some cruel men

had kidnapped her

and bought her steak dinners

in exchange for sex.

Twenty-five years later,

I still can't let the memory

go.

I have now come to understand,

that some people don't survive

in our society,

because they're too good, too naïve.

I now trust mostly God

and that's all I can believe.

Lazy Bones

At a halfway house,

where I once found a bed,

there lived a young woman,

who lived there half dead.

We all called her lazy.

She wouldn't do chores.

This made us all "crazy"

condemning her more.

She slept every day,

and we mumbled

our threats.

After a while we used

childish attacks.

Refusing to go to the workshop each day,

she lay in her bed

watching the rain.

The vigilant counselors

tried this way and that

to make her

comply like all of the rest.

Then suddenly,

one night,

she

died

of

bone cancer.

No one

called

her

"lazy bones"

anymore.

Touching the Magic Screen

TV preachers with

plastic smiles

and

greedy creeds

coax and demand,

as

the

hapless patients

on

the

unit

touch the magic screen

or

communicate

with subjective signs.

The

secret "second coming"

comes

again

and

again-

These ungodly delusions

are

soothing

to

a

rootless

toothless

soul.

A Day in Hell for the Mentally Ill

Forgotten residents

drink

tap water coffee

and

smoke

hand me down cigarettes

salvaged

from the

floor.

They walk their

demons

down

dark

dreary

halls,

while their silent

screaming

(drones on) within

within their souls.

Each day residents' half

competent doctors

ask

their sanity questions

like

"Who is President?"

(as if

it matters at all)

Then,

when

the nurses'

medications

are given,

the patients bite their own tongues

and wander like sheep.

And so the residents' only

releases

are

recycled Spam

and

a

mind numbing sleep

from which they pray to God they will never

awaken.

Alone Again

Mad upon a faceless sea,

they wander

down

electric streets,

where coincidences

are

Almighty signs.

They recycle food and

relevant newspaper clippings

from garbage cans

along the way,

as they

march up

and

down

the boulevard

searching for

the (knowing)

pop stars

of

MTV.

In time,

some

nervous police officers

escort

them

to

those

bleak institutions,

past the grounds

where

nobody

walks.

And for their sins,

they endure

thorazine shots

in

spread-eagled beds

until

they

crash.

Depressed

and

Alone

Again.

All Those Years Ago

Awakening

back into

his disease,

a tortured mind

pilfers

a jar of instant coffee

and

brews a tepid cup

from the lavatory faucet.

He then

limps

down the long dreary corridor

stooping

down

repeatedly

to

pick up

cigarette butts

from the dull tile floor.

Then he

arouses the tech

behind a reinforced glass window

and

successfully pleads

for a solitary stick match.

For the rest of the day,

he slowly paces in the hall

waiting for the promised pass

to the commissary.

He numbly rehearses

the words he will use

to convince his psychiatrist

that a pass is all right.

When he finally receives his prize,

he wanders the grounds,

but he is caught leaving the scene

headed for town.

When he is escorted back

to the "acute unit",

he intentionally freaks out

and receives a shot of thorazine.

As he sleeps, he escapes his mind

and the time,

yet again. I know this story is true

because the "he" was "me"

all those many years ago.

After the Crashing

The manic mind

explodes,

uncontrollably focused on obsessions that grow

like

chanting numbers,

rummaging through dumpsters,

and

scribbling nonsensical rhyme.

But

then, when

the

inevitable

crashing

at

last

subsides,

images more comprehensible

form

in the

expanded mind.

And it matters

not

that nobody listens,

because

it's God

the mind discovers

in

its

transparent

soul.

Who could ask for more?

Humility is the Cost

Conceived in arrogance

and grown from

madness,

my art was

born

from

pain and

loss.

But

now

I create

from the

higher mind,

wherein

humility is the

law;

together with

a

calm

isolated existence

that allows

me

          JOHN FREDERICK ZURN

to write

wildly free

with one foot in my dull routine

and the other foot

with God.

But if I

trip

and

fall

on my resurrected

ego again,

then I must

slay it

immediately,

or I will

die

in the noisy crowd

again.

Behind the Metal Doors

I left my student yesterday

within a house of pain.

He always seemed to trust in me

but now he'd gone insane.

They told me in a month or so

he would be okay.

But when I saw him staggering,

the truth got in the way.

His face was grim and strangely cold

with spit caked in his hair.

He wore pajamas stained and torn,

and no one seemed to care.

When I tried to kid with him,

he wasn't really there.

When I asked him how he felt,

he only sat and stared.

I left him in his world that night

behind the metal doors.

His mind had once again returned

to madness like before.

In my heart I said good-bye

and wasn't really sure,

If God would heal the agony

that doctors couldn't cure.

The Glowing Embers of Desire

Oh Lord, I'm just a restless heart

who still trusts in emotion.

My feelings fester like my thoughts,

so motives seem important.

Then pride cloaked in self-righteousness

points out the faults of others.

Retreating into selfishness,

all love and peace are smothered.

Oh Lord, I'm not a wicked soul,

yet every day seems longer.

Your love has taught me self-control,

but still, at times, I falter.

The glowing embers of desire

flare up with every problem.

Then haunting, shifting memories,

rise up and soon take over.

Oh Lord, I'm not a patient man,

so life is rush and worry.

My day evolves around demands

that bring no joy or meaning.

So, Lord, I sense that only you

can free me from this prison.

The outer world and all I knew

are shadows and illusions.

A Sweet Surrender

A sweet surrender from within

begins to still my mind.

Thoughts dissolve and love descends

passing into quiet.

A tender stream of loneliness

is sweet like summer rain.

A calm and gentle emptiness

bring God and love again.

As meditation takes control,

an inner presence lingers.

My mind, so softly, sweetly goes,

and love and beauty enter.

A subtle silence fills with grace

beyond all thoughts and feelings.

The moment is a holy peace,

and death is soon defeated.

But then the moment reaches out

to capture my emotions.

Time sets in and haunting doubts

collapse and search for meaning.

Desires surface like a dream

constricting love and faith.

Then my plans and memories

bring back the world again.

Blessed Be God Forever

If in my heart I seek to know

your will in times of sorrow;

but you are teaching me to grow,

so onward I must travel:

Blessed Be God Forever.

If deep within my weary mind

I call to you in prayer;

but you await the perfect time,

so I must linger here:

Blessed Be God Forever.

If I wait with idle hands,

yet work cannot be found;

and my soul can't understand

because it feels cast down:

Blessed Be God forever.

If every deed is ground to dust,

and hope and faith are strained;

but still you tell me I must trust

and do my best each today:

Blessed Be God Forever.

If the silence cracks and breaks,

and worry stalks my dreams;

and loneliness I cannot fake

because I'm lost in need:

Blessed Be God Forever.

Yet if I fail to win a place,

but you are satisfied;

and all I have is love and grace

to lead me through this life:

Blessed Be God Forever.

Blessed Be God Today.

Always in the Darkest Times

All peaceful joy and certainty

begin to fall away.

This moment of despondency

brings back both time and space.

The inner silence strains, then fails,

as anxious thoughts rush in.

Confusion and a shattered truth

soon overwhelm belief.

A suffocating fear and doubt

bewilder thought and feeling.

The sense of death invades my soul

attacking hope and purpose.

Peace and solace disappoint,

and every sign is morbid.

All that lives seems far away,

and God seems even farther.

Yet God exists beyond belief,

And He is Light primeval.

When faith and hope are driven out,

She is the Love forever.

Always in the darkest times,

despair distorts emotion.

God moves through the whole of life

regardless of perception.

Every Trial is Grace

My thoughts feel cold and cracked today

like brittle autumn leaves.

My heart dries up and I'm afraid,

and life is misery.

My mind projects so many fears;

I'm paralyzed and broken .

Alone within my grim despair,

I wander through emotion.

My hopes fade into memory,

and faith creates no peace.

Now courage is the only thing

that brings my soul relief.

Each day is like the one before,

and every dream is crushed.

I seek to find an open door,

so God and love will come.

But then a calm, at last, returns,

and tensions pass away.

If God asks patience, I will serve,

and He will lead the way.

Suffering and wisdom come,

no matter what I face.

Courage leads to joy and love,

and every trial is grace.

I Shall Live a Life of Courage

I shall live a life of courage

facing hardships with resolve.

Every burden I shall carry

seeking out the Lord for help.

Faith will lead me far from danger

filling me with strength and prayer.

I will overcome my anger

rising up beyond my fears.

Love will lead me through the forest

wafting through the midnight air.

Light will be my source of comfort

guiding me beyond despair.

Every future I abandon

giving up my need to know.

Lost to God I now surrender

all the things I can't control.

I shall live a life of freedom

calling on Almighty God.

I will pass beyond my reason

climbing toward the rising sun.

Death is but an eerie shadow

lurking on some foreign shore.

God alone my heart will follow

trusting Him to take me home.

Lord, I Pray For Independence

Oh Lord, I'm still an anxious child

who clamors for attention.

My sense of self-esteem relies

on every thought and action.

The people that I meet each day

must be my friend or ally.

When others don't reciprocate,

I feel I am a failure.

This childish attitude toward life

believes in perfect friendship.

Still stuck within my wrong and right,

I seek to find acceptance.

If honor puffs me up with pride,

my heart ascends with laughter.

But if I feel the blame inside,

my day is a disaster.

Lord, I pray for independence

free from all my childish thoughts.

Giving up my expectations,

I will see your love in all.

I now surrender attitudes

that thrive on recognition.

My spirit yearns to follow you

in quiet resignation.

Oh Lord, I Pray for Simple Joy

Oh Lord, I pray for simple joy

and quiet conversation.

I ask to be at peace within

and need your grace and mercy.

In gratitude, I praise your name

and rest beside your meadow.

In solitude, I sit and wait,

and feel your light and shadow.

My Lord, I pray for simple needs,

so I may know contentment.

I ask for true humility

and long for your acceptance.

With fortitude, I cling to you

with quiet resignation.

With thankfulness, I worship you

in silent meditation.

My Lord I pray for simple thoughts ,

so I may find your wisdom.

I ask for you to touch my heart

and lead me to your kingdom.

In loneliness, I cry to you

and yearn for you to answer.

In happiness I sing to you ,

and life is joy and laughter.

Every Fear is Slowly Dying

My heart finds joy, beating faster,

safely lost among the flowers.

Intuition dawns then lingers

like a fragrant, summer shower.

Thought and feeling merge together

free from every selfishness.

Compassion and a silent power

overwhelm my loneliness.

Awareness builds an open sky

steeped in cosmic mystery.

Every fear of death is dying

lost to faith in God instead.

Energy pervades existence

deep within and all around.

Everywhere my soul is singing

free to merge with love and sound.

But still this landscape comes and goes,

And I feel separation.

From deep within my heart and soul,

I seek God in creation.

Contentment is the toughest task

when patience turns to hurry.

Attachment is a living death

that leads to every worry.

The Edge of Dawn

The edge of dawn is doubt and fear,

as darkness still controls.

An emptiness and nothingness

engulfs both faith and hope.

Each moment feels like desert sand,

and every peak is flat.

A world of sorrow overwhelms,

and life is living death.

The edge of dawn is trapped and blind,

so time grinds through the moment.

Thoughts and feelings flood the space

until the heart is broken.

Prayer becomes an empty motion

stuck within a form and name.

Service lacks all joy and purpose

drowning in a sea of change.

The secret dawn may come again,

so patience waits with courage.

No fevered thoughts will conjure it,

and scattered thoughts are worthless.

The God of Love and Light is real,

yet life is cold and shallow.

The darkness withers every path,

and every peace is hollow.

The God Called I Am

I am the force that drives the world-

its swarming crowds, its scattered few.

I bend the sky to hold the earth

and shape the eager, spilling stream.

My power twists and churns the sea

beneath my restless, magic moon.

I scorch and melt the mountain stone

that belches up above the clouds.

I am the dark medieval forest-

its ancient dawns and mystic nights.

I hear the song of bird and flower

chanting in my golden fields.

My breath pours out the wind and rain,

so fragrant pines can bless the earth.

I spare the sun from crashing down

and draw the movement of the stars.

I am the wisdom of creation-

its primal myths, its holy saints.

I reach behind the world of matter

raising up or casting out.

My life and death are endless dramas

written for the cosmic stage.

I see the world before I made it

drifting through eternal mind.

I am the energy called light-

this love, this love, this love, this love.

I hide within the sage and fool

behind the world of right and wrong.

My love and grace hear simple prayers,

and patience is my dearest friend.

I live and hide in everyone,

but I am God, forever light.

About The Author

John Frederick Zurn has faced the challenges of bipolar and anxiety disorder his entire adult life. Over the years he has gradually learned ways to improve his overall health through medication, physical exercise, meditation and creative writing - all vital to his long term recovery. His transformation through spiritual discovery has given his life a greater sense of purpose. John had a 35 year career as a teacher and counselor. Now retired, he spends his days writing poems and stories. Born in upstate New York, he has an M.A. in English from Western Illinois University. He and his wife, Donna, have been married for over forty years.

"Contact" John on his website

https://www.portalstoinnerdimensions.com/

Facebook: "Friend" John

https://www.facebook.com/writerjohnfzurn/

Books by John Frederick Zurn

Autobiographical

Mental Illness Experiences

The End Justifies the Pain

The Promise of Long Term Recovery

Metamorphosis: from Mental Illness to Spiritual Awakening

Spiritual Experiences

This Moment Called God

Passing Through the Dream

One Hundred Devotional Poems

Poems of Hope and Inspiration

Fiction

Sojourners Through Time

Expedition to the Northland

Unexpected Pilgrims

Humor

The Comedy in Everyday Life

Don't miss out!

Visit the website below and you can sign up to receive emails whenever John Frederick Zurn publishes a new book. There's no charge and no obligation.

https://books2read.com/r/B-A-IHPT-GFLEC

BOOKS 2 READ

Connecting independent readers to independent writers.

Did you love *The Bipolar Challenge*? Then you should read *The End Justifies the Pain : Writings About Mental Health*[1] by John Frederick Zurn!

[2]

John chronicles some of his bipolar episode experiences, both in-patient and outpatient;, and how he has achieved long term recovery. He details the process of identifying the appropriate medication and the importance of consistent usage. He identifies a variety of coping skills - how to develop and use them. John then delves into how creative expression can channel thoughts and emotions in useful and constructive ways, psychological and spiritual. As examples of John's creative process, he includes 2 of his short stories and 17 poems.

Read more at https://www.portalstoinnerdimensions.com/.

---

1. https://books2read.com/u/md68RW

2. https://books2read.com/u/md68RW